1

CHILD & DOG Safety

A resource for dog owners, parents and teachers.

JEANETTE GRONER

This book is dedicated
to my husband Tom and my daughters
Tessa, Dana, Anique and Heidi.
I could have never done this without your support.

Illustrations done by Dana and Tessa

CONTENT

Chantry's Stormy Days

A dog who has served his community by searching for the lost and comforting those in need.

1   INTRODUCTION

Man's best friend is often a child's best friend. When facing tough times the family dog is the first one to hear the thoughts of a child. A dog will always listen patiently to the stories children tell. Parents know how special a dog can be to their son or daughter. Scientists have come to the same conclusion. Pre-adolescent children ages 9 thru 12 show statistically higher self esteem and empathy compared to their peers without a family dog. Dogs are of greatest influence in those years than at any other stage in their lives. (Bierer, 2000) Special needs children in preschool follow direction better when they perform tasks with a trained dog nearby. They function better in class with a dog around, then when they are by themselves or accompanied by a person or stuffed animal. The children need fewer prompts to complete a task even though you would think that the dog is a distraction. A dog helps enhance children's cognitive and gross motor skills. (Ghee, 2009) All over the world scientists come to the same conclusion. The interaction between animals and people can be very powerful. It provides a context which improves communication, elevates self-confidence, reduces symptoms of diseases and improves quality of life. (Dimitrijević I., 2009, Serbia)

I grew up in The Netherlands where the dog, compared to the USA, has a different social status within society. But when it comes to children, there is no difference. Each child seeks attention and unconditional love no matter where he or she lives.

Dogs provide these needs more often than we realize. But the relationship between a child and a dog does have its challenges. A dog is an animal. A child is human. Dog language is complex. It includes different components which a young child is not able to observe. For example a dog is not always friendly when he wags his tail. Components which determine the mood a dog is in are: context, muscle tone, overall body posture and subtle movement of the eyes, ears, mouth and head. Young children are not able to understand the subtleties in a dog. They can not distinguish between warning signals or friendly gestures. As adults we have to step in and keep our children safe.

In the early nineties the United Kingdom developed a successful program. It became the British Oscar & Rufus project which soon thereafter was implemented in The Netherlands. Certified instructors accompanied with their therapy dog started to teach the project in public schools.

Many years later the program was refined and now is called the Snuffel College. The program is based on teaching children compassion and dog safety skills. I became a certified instructor (1994) and my dog Nikki joined me in class. When I brought Nikki into the classroom it was a great experience to see the anticipation on the faces of the children. Before they would meet Nikki they had to learn skills on how to appropriately   greet and care for a dog. After two class sessions I would bring in Nikki as to help the children practice with a real dog. The biggest challenge to them was to stand still like a tree when Nikki came close to greet them. Their whole body just wanted to wiggle of excitement.

When I became a handler and instructor of search and rescue dogs in the early nineties, I came across a different aspect of dog safety. It was the challenge to train our highly socially driven working dogs to correctly work around children. We were involved in search missions where a child was lost or had run away. The biggest challenge was to find a child who was deeply afraid of a dog and would hide. As a dog owner and trainer I realized that it was my responsibility to train my dogs to respect the boundaries of a child. I then recognized both sides of the issue. One side is the dog owner who does not have children. On the other side is the parent and dog owner. We have to teach our children safety skills but as dog owners we also have to take responsibility to enhance the social skills in our dogs.

Through the years I continued teaching safety skills to families. I now am a mom and have come full circle in understanding all facets of child and dog interaction. There are different programs which can help you as parent understand how to teach your child dog safety. But the problem with programs like *Blue Dog* and *Be A Tree* is that they only focus on the child. We can not put the responsibility solely on our children. As adults we have to take the time to learn how a dog communicates, spend time training and take time to socialize. If you own a dog bring awareness to the community about the importance of breeding socially sound dogs. Due to puppy mills and irresponsible breeders we are starting to face dogs which are unable to appropriately connect with people. They are unable to deal with stress and react instead of think. Due to poor body awareness, they panic when touched or are so insensitive that they do not respect physical boundaries. Dogs which are separated from their mom and littermates too early in life and lack bite inhibition skills. You have to conclude that child and dog safety starts with us adults and not with the child.

Here I am at work with dogs to build socialization skills. We are at the dog daycare facility of Rogue Valley Veterinary Hospital in Rockford, MI. www.roguevalleyvet.com

As a mom of four daughters, child safety instructor and dog behavior specialist I have grown a passion for child safety. For this reason I developed **STORM™**. The mission of STORM™ is to create an awareness of what parents and dog owners can do to keep children safe around dogs. We can also change the view of breeders when parents and/or dog owners become more responsible in dog ownership and select the right dog for the family. The law of supply and demand will enforce change. When it comes to selecting bloodlines breeders will start choosing brains and physical health over beauty. STORM™ provides tools to help teach your child dog safety. STORM™ stands for:

- **S**afety skills for children
- **T**raining plan for your dog
- **O**bservation skills to learn dog language
- **R**esponsibility for parents
- **M**eet & greet for dogs on the street.

Our black Labrador Storm inspired me to name this project after him. He is a retired search and rescue dog. He served his community by my husbands' side for 9 years and has become our daughters' confidant. His ability to function within our family is unique. Chantry's Stormy Days is a high spirited working dog who has reached the grandpa stage in life. Yet he is calm, content and a cuddle addict around the kids. Dogs often never have an issue with children around them. But if you look into the facts on dog bite incidents we need to wake up as a society.

I have trained dogs since 1987 and started my instructing career in 1991 with the Dutch ASPCA during College. I mostly rehabilitated shelter dogs into society. Our dog obedience classes were focused on owners of adopted shelter dogs. We helped them build a relationship with their dog based on leadership, mutual respect and trust. I moved to the USA in 1997 and continued my career in dog training and behavior modification. Through my profession I have encountered the worst. Yet it is such a special gift to be able to have a dog share your household. It is heart-warming to hear about hero-dogs who help their family through tough times. The power of touch and a faithful canine friend in a child's life can help autistic children or children with SID come out of their shell. The world will open up to children when a dog comes into their lives with whom they can connect. They feel safe again during the trials of life. The unconditional love that you receive from a dog can't be put into words. It literally saves lives. I'll never forget the moment my youngest daughter held a 3 week old puppy in her arms. Feeling this warm puppy in her hands made her melt, creating a peace within her that I had not ever seen before.

May this book help you better understand this very special animal and the dynamics of child & dog interaction. We are not made to do life alone. Dogs have filled hearts where there was emptiness. Their role in society can not be ignored. Lets take on the responsibility to keep our children safe and build a socially healthy dog population…..

"Everything that lives, lives not alone nor for itself"
William Blake

2   FACTS

The CDC and US Humane Society gathered statistics to map out dog bite incidents. According to a recent report, each year in the USA 4.5 million people are bitten by a dog of which roughly 800,000 will need medical attention. Of those numbers half are children under the age of 12 years old. Interestingly the highest occurrence of bite incidents happens with the family dog within the home or on the owners' property. Adults were not actively involved through supervising the dog and child. The bite incident was most often a direct result of the actions of the child. A 5 year review of pediatric dog bite incidents came with interesting facts. During this study period five hundred fifty-one patients were treated in the emergency department after suffering dog bite injuries during the study period. Study facts:

(Kaye and Colleagues, Philadelphia 2009) :

- The majority of injuries (62.8 percent) were sustained by male children.

- Dog bite injuries were most prevalent during the months of June and July (24.1 percent).

- The majority of victims, 51%, were grade school-aged children (6 to 12 years).

- Preschoolers (2 to 5 years; 24.0 percent)
- Teenagers (13 to 18 years; 20.5 percent)
- Infants (birth to 1 year; 4.5 percent).
- Injuries sustained by infants and preschoolers often involved the face (53.5 percent), whereas older children sustained injuries to the extremities (60.7 percent).

Due to the bite incident statistics the government is now stepping in. The government has written Breed Specific Legislation which regulates your right to own or not own a specific dog. But the problem of this legislation is that it's based solely on the breed or "type" of dog - not the responsibility of an owner. Legislators may even attempt to ban a breed completely as some countries have done. The Dutch government has now adjusted their legislation. For many years Pitbull type dogs were discriminated against and banned in society. But in 2009 the Dutch government came to the realization that banning this breed did not decrease the bite incidents in the country. As of January of 2009, any type of dog which is involved in a bite incident can now be confiscated. There is no longer an obsessive focus on the Pitbull type. (RAD article 350 & 425) The fact is that all kinds of breeds are to blame, even the loved Labrador and golden retrievers are on the bite incident list. We are facing breed legislation due to irresponsible breeders, puppy mills which raise mentally unstable dogs and uninformed dog owners. So how do we keep our children safe? Do not make an impulsive buy and bring a dog in the house without first doing thorough research. Responsible breeders will use puppy temperament tests to help potential owners understand the puppies better.

Rescue organizations will use special temperament tests for older dogs to evaluate their adoptability. Throughout the world different behavior tests are used and refined. The Socially Acceptable Behavior test has been used by the Dutch government to enforce responsible breeding with certain breeds. From Rottweiler to Jack Russell terrier, the test is required before a dog is used for breeding. The Dutch Rottweiler population has actually improved due to the required behavior test. It is a fact that through responsible breeding, socialization awareness, dog training and informed owners the dog population can change. We have to focus on breeding dogs with strong nerve strength and a healthy central nervous system. A nervous system which is balanced with a healthy ability to process stress and problem solve. This balance results in dogs which do not purely react to their environment. They will have the ability to think through a situation without a fight-flight reaction. (Kagan 1987) Dogs with a balanced mind can learn that a touch or hug, without warning, is not a threat. Family dogs should be capable of learning these skills. But the unfortunate fact is that we deal with many family pet dogs who are not the right match. They have poor nerve strength and are filled with anxieties.

"Breed not a savage dog, nor permit a loose stairway."
Talmud

3   CHOOSE THE RIGHT DOG FOR YOUR FAMILY

It is not an easy task to find the right dog for your family. There are many factors within the decision making process. The worst you can do for your family is to make an impulsive and uninformed decision in buying a dog. Take your time. Your dog may be with you for more than 10 years. There are several steps involved which form a responsible and informed decision on finding a family dog;

a) Determine the needs of the family
b) Decide between a puppy of older dog
c) Use the CHILD approach to gather facts.

In your search for a dog you will come across different temperament test. They are used by breeders and other professionals to gather information about the dog. My experience in testing dogs comes from different backgrounds. I have tested countless dogs for adoptability, work skills, behavior modification evaluations and puppy tests. Each test has a unique component aimed at the specific goal of the test itself. Humane Society and animal shelters throughout the country use tests like

MeetYourMatch™ or Asses-A-Pet™. They are great tools if conducted by experience dog trainers. For beginning dog owners I put the CHILD approach together. It is not a temperament test but it informs the potential dog owner about what to look for in a family dog. It is more an educational tool than a temperament test used by professionals.
CHILD is an acronym for:

- ✓ **C**haracter; which dog character matches the needs of your family.
- ✓ **H**andling; what type of handling does the dog have to withstand.
- ✓ **I**mpulse; what is the level of nerve strength you are looking for in a dog.
- ✓ **L**ineage; the advantages of knowing the breed or parents of the dog.
- ✓ **D**rives; what motivate a dog and what is the best fit for your family.

Family needs

The first consideration is to evaluate the need of your family. Do you have children with medical needs like allergies? Exposure to cats and dogs during childhood has actually been linked to a lower risk of developing allergies.(Mandhane, 2009) But if one of your children already has allergies it may not be a problem to have a dog in the house. Consult your pediatrician for more information as a new trend within the dog world is growing. It is very popular to mix breeds known for their special coat

27

structure. Breeds like the Poodle or Shi-Tsu are often used. Waterdogs are also very popular for this very reason. They do not shed as most dogs do, which prevents exposure to allergen. The unique coat structure will need different attention through special grooming. These mixed dogs come in all sizes. They often make great family pets as the poodle character seems to be very prevalent. They are friendly and never grow up. If they are born with a responsible breeder and well socialized they will be very play-full and friendly. But these high energy dogs may not be the best pet if you have a child with ADD traits. In this case you have to specifically find a calm dog and not a dog which is sensitive to its surroundings. Another thing to consider is the age of your children. Having a baby and a puppy at the same time is going to be a challenge which you may not be ready for. As toddlers, babies or preschoolers love to explore a puppy will be the exact same way. A puppy needs as much time as a toddler or they will get into trouble. Potty training, socialization and puppy proofing the house is all very time consuming. Proofing your house includes setting up a kid-free zone. This room, crate or kennel is a special area where your dog can retreat to for a nap. Even if you do not have children, a dog needs a place in the home where he or she can feel safe and is able to rest. It is a place where no one can trip over the dog. When guests come to visit your dog has a way to retreat. Is your home able to house a dog? Each family has unique challenges. Full-time jobs, fearful children, home associations and insurance regulations are all to be considered when you choose the right match for your family. Evaluate the needs of the whole family and the community you live in.

We all have a responsibility to our community. Not everyone will agree with me on this. But we have all been put on earth with a deeper purpose of which one is to not look only after our own needs but consider the needs of people around us. I take this very seriously. In my younger years I had a dog in the home which was trained very irresponsibly by its owner. Wrong training methods combined with a child in the neighborhood who loved to tease the dog resulted in a recipe for disaster. The moment the leash was snapped on this dog, he turned into a dangerous animal which would bite anyone that would come too close. If he was loose he would only tolerate adults but children were never his favorite. We had come to the conclusion that this dog had become a danger to the community and we euthanized him. It was by no means an easy decision though it was the right one. I learned a lot from him through his years with us, especially how dogs can perceive children. Out of pure necessity I became very skilled in reading the language of a dog when children were around. This dog still has a special place in my heart. He was a product of wrong breeding and ignorance in training KNPV* bite work skills. I personally love the Schutzhund, IPO** and KNPV training, but only a skilled few know how to select a pup and train it to be a perfect protection dog without jeopardizing the dogs' social skills.

* *KNPV (Koninklijke Nederlandse Politiebonden Vereniging) An organization through which handlers and dogs compete in police dog skills. It includes tracking, obstacle courses, obedience, bite work and scent detection skills.*
** *IPO (Internationale Prüfungs Ordnung) and Schutzhund are organizations through which you can compete with your dog in bite work skills, obedience and tracking. More dogs are able to compete in IPO/Schutzhund than in KNPV.*

Puppy vs. Older dog. Adopting an older mature dog can give you more information where a puppy needs time to develop. Humane societies and shelters often have trained people on staff who have the ability to test dogs before they are ready for adoption. They test a dog by using a point system. This point system will make it easier to match a dog with the right family. These tests are conducted in a sterile environment by professional evaluators.

They will test the dog or pup on the following:

> ➤ Social skills
> ➤ Resource guarding
> ➤ Kennel presentation
> ➤ Touch sensitivity
> ➤ Stranger test
> ➤ Baby and toddler test
> ➤ Dog to dog test
> ➤ Nerve strength

The advantage of choosing a rescue organization over a shelter is that their animals often live in foster families. They are not kenneled in a stressful shelter environment. Fostered dogs are already functioning within a family before they are ready to go to a new home. The foster parents will be able to give you detailed information on the dog's behavior. Above all else refrain from buying a dog from a puppy-mill or a pet store. Though some were lucky in buying a healthy dog there, most often this will not be the case. Mental and physical problems are very common in these dogs. It is likely impossible to trace back where the dog came from let alone meet any ancestors of the pup to evaluate the bloodline for health or mental issues.

CHILD

As there are tools for experienced dog trainers to evaluate dogs, I have put together a tool for soon-to-be dog owners. Using the CHILD method (Character, Handling, Impulse control, Lineage, Drives) you will be able to make a more informed decision. The history of an older dog may not always be very clear. The beauty is that a dog may not function within a certain family but blossom within another. Adopting a pup or older dog can be very rewarding. Through the CHILD approach you will be able to make a breed selection and get a deeper understanding how to select a dog for your family.

Character

Character is the set of qualities that makes a dog distinct. Character is doing what's right when nobody's looking. When you are interested in adopting an older dog you most likely will first evaluate his character. What distinctions are you looking for in an older dog? Calm attitude, a busy bee which needs lots of exercise or a dog who will greet you with a friendly gentle nudge? Unfortunately the dogs you meet at shelters may not always portray themselves the way they truly are. I speak for the dogs which do not thrive in a kennel environment due to fear and stress. They feel cornered and threatened especially with strangers staring at them several times a day. Many great shelter dogs are passed by due to this very reason. It is very tough to make a judgment call only based on one meeting with a dog at the shelter. Take time to talk with the staff and ask for any behavior evaluations they might have done. A dog often needs time to heal and settle in when you bring him into your home. I strongly believe that character evolves through time as your dog grows with your family. Often after the right match is found it takes 2-3 months before the dog has settled in. It is an adjustment for the family as well, and it takes time for a dog to fit in and become acquainted with new routines. So you may have the perfect dog in mind, with the exact character traits that you are looking for, it still is going to take time for family and dog to unite as you get to know each other. Although a dog evolves as it gets to know his new family, you can look for distinct character traits and consult with the shelter staff or foster families. With children at home you are looking for a dog with a character which does not respond excessively to movement and has a high social connection with people. Professional dog trainers in your area can help you determine the subtle character traits of your dog.

I will never forget when I adopted my first dog. A one year old German Shepherd Nikki. She clearly needed the time to learn to trust people but after her first two months with me she started to blossom in life and became the best family member you can imagine. She was a reject of society. With a pedigree supporting her purebred status, she was still clearly considered the ugly duckling among her breed. Her ears were floppy and her hind legs were very dysfunctional. But she was my best friend and when I became mom, she became my children's best friend. She accompanied me at public schools while I taught children to safely interact with her. She passed a therapy dog test allowing her to visit the classrooms with me. But the first month with her was a time of growth for both her and me. I'll never forget that one afternoon. She was sleeping on her blanket in the living room. In a deep sleep seemingly unaware of her surroundings I walked by with a trash bag. Well things changed rapidly. Within a second she was standing on all fours and growled at me. I stood very still trying to figure out what I had done to upset her. It must have been the sound of the trash bag that I had tried to open up. As her response was clearly based on fear I did not reprimand her.

I stayed quiet and let her adrenaline level subside to the point that she could think clear again. She then started to investigate the situation and concluded that nothing was there to cause a threat. Immediately her whole tail started to wag loosely and her whole body relaxed. We both learned a lot from that incident. I clearly had scared her with the noise of the trash bag. She never again had issues with trash bags. She was a very special dog, accompanied me on urban search and rescue training drills with the Red Cross. When I moved to the USA she flew across the Atlantic Ocean with me. She developed from a dog who was scared of everything, to a dog which served her community and welcomed my daughters in the family when they were born.

Nikki past away of heart failure when she was 12 years old. She taught me all about life and second chances, about faithfulness and unconditional love. Above all about patience and to give a dog a second chance in life. Allow your puppy or older dog time to grow in your family. To adopt an older dog is something very special. But you have to do some homework to make sure that it is the right fit with your children. Character builds through time. But it has to be based on a healthy balanced mind which is able to process life without immediately jumping into survival mode.

Handling

When you meet a dog for the first time in the adoption process observe how this dog responds to being handled. At most Humane Society and shelters they test this extensively. But as we are all uniquely made and have our strengths and weaknesses, a dog may respond slightly different to you than to an evaluator in a sterile test environment. Keeping child safety in mind, you want to look for a dog which does not react with a flight or fight instinct when being touched without warning. Some dogs may not allow you to touch their paws or panic when they are restraint. How does the dog respond when you look straight at him? Some dogs are very unforgiving and feel threatened easily while other dogs simply look away and avoid conflict. You want a dog which trusts people and is not skittish. Keep in mind that children are the master of touching a dog inappropriately. They sometimes sit on a dog or may start a stare down contest for fun. Take your time when you meet a potential new dog to connect with him and get to know him. Do not allow anyone to rush you into making a decision. Preferably do not bring your children to the first meeting with a potential new family member. It adds chaos and emotional pressure to the scene as each dog really is cute! ☺

Impulse Control

Ideally you want a dog which can be calm, patient and control his impulses. You would be surprised how fast a dog can respond when he sees a cookie in a child's hand, or an unsecured hotdog on a plate. Dogs which react without thinking to the environment around them can be of risk as they most likely need extra training to respect your children and not literally use your child as a doormat in order to satisfy their needs. Some herding dogs have a very intense response to movement. This can be hard to control or re-direct. Terriers are often very independent and have a low impulse control. As they can be very feisty, often breeders remove them from the mom at an early age. This does not allow mom to teach the pup about personal space and to control their impulses. If you really like Terriers take your time to find a breeder who leaves the pups with the mom as long as possible. Jack Russell terriers are very popular. But they have become jumpy little guys who are very intense. There are breeders who still focus on qualities like nerve strength. But you have to take the time to find them. Some breeds have such ingrained social skills that they are unable to control themselves with people around. They greet people inappropriately by excessive jumping. Take your time to find the breeder who understands your need and takes time to listen to you. Dogs with a low control over their impulses will not focus well and are easily distracted. They may be very sensitive to sounds and react to their surroundings. The more impulsive a dog is, the harder it will be to have him around children who are very active and chaotic themselves.

Lineage

Breed or mix, it does not matter much unless you are looking for very specific traits in a dog. First and foremost, what is the reason for bringing a dog into your family? Your family may be looking for a companion dog with abilities to excel in a particular area. Here are some ideas;

- ➤ Schutzhund, KNPV, IPO or Search&Rescue require dogs with skills which you will mostly find in the AKC Working dog group or Herding group. Often you will see dogs from the Sporting group in SAR.
- ➤ Therapy dog require dogs with skills which you will find in any kind of AKC group. Therapy dogs have to be well socialized dogs with strong nerve strength to deal with new situations.
- ➤ Hunting skills can be found in the AKC Sporting dog group, Hound group or Terrier group depending what your hunting target is.
- ➤ Competitive sports like agility, flyball, treibball or lure courses can be done with a lot of different types of dogs. Most often you will

> see dogs compete from the Herding group, Working group or Terrier group.
> ➤ Herding and/or guarding skills for life stock will mostly occur with dogs in the AKC Working group and Herding group.
> ➤ Sled dogs can be found in the AKC Working dog group.

There is an advantage in choosing a purebred. As they have been selected for many years (sometimes more than a century) you can predict easier what kind of dog your pup grows into. But mixed-breed dogs can also be very special and excel in sports. If you are purely looking for a family companion then focus on looking for different qualities. It makes a difference in choosing a bloodline which is not selected for work skills but mainly for show or family. Working lines have a higher need for mental and physical exercise. They have to be mentally or physically challenged on continuing bases. If you do not have enough time for the dog problem behaviors will start to emerge. Dogs which are bred for work also tend to be more possessive over toys. They need a strong leader in the family to learn to respect and follow. Dogs which are bred for companionship only, will make a better fit overall.

They are easier content with life and are able to connect better with children.

Guard dogs can be a great family companion as long as their guarding instinct is not based on fear or anti-social behavior. Dogs with a low pack drive will be weary about strangers and may only connect with one person in the family. They will not respect children. Researching the lineage of a dog will provide information that can be of great value. Medical information, behavior problems, genetic disorders or titles can all be traced back with a bloodline. Even with mixed breeds you might be able to trace back the family line.

The Catahoula Leopard dog, can be a great guard dog but due to the wrong reasons. They have a lack of pack drive. Not an easy breed to have around young children. Though they look REALLY cute! ☺

Your veterinarian or dog trainer will be able to help. If you did choose a specific breed then visit a gathering of breed enthusiasts. These gatherings are a great place to see the dog at work in its natural surroundings. For example you may love the Jack Russell terrier. I agree that they are very cute. But when you witness their hunt skills, detecting rodents by digging them up, then don't be surprised when the day of truth arrives. It is the day when your Jack Russell puppy is digging out your precious petunias in the garden. And you can only blame yourself for not preventing the whole situation. Purebred dogs have been selected for over centuries to perform specific tasks. To understand these tasks and learn about the strengths and weaknesses of a breed, you will know more what to expect when you bring a dog into your home. A trained eye is able to determine the background of mixed breeds. There are actually DNA tests available to determine the background of a mixed breed. Breed specific research is a great way to get to know your future puppy.

Drives
What motivates a dog to chase a Frisbee around? Yet some dogs will not even look at the Frisbee. Why does one dog run away when scared and the

other attack? Why does one Labrador see a tennis ball as an equivalent to a pacifier and another Labrador has no clue what to do with it? There are different drives in a dog and one can be more prevalent within the dog than the other. The *prey drive* within a dog will display behaviors that are based on hunting. You do not want a dog with a high prey drive if you have children. These dogs tend to chase anything that moves and get the reward out of grabbing and shaking the toy.. In extreme cases they will stalk, stare at their potential prey and even kill it. Rabbits, squirrels or cats are often the victim as they move fast and trigger the prey drive in a dog. A dog with a high prey drive can display these behaviors only with toys or other animals around them. But if it gets out of hand these traits can become a danger to your child. Play time is no longer innocent. The dog will become increasingly rough in play through pouncing and grabbing you. The *pack drive* involves a dog's connection to other dogs and people. If you have children you want a dog with a high pack drive as they will have better social skills. These dogs really enjoy being with people. If you stand next to this dog he or she will choose to be close instead of ignoring you. You can observe the difference when you see an owner with a Labrador on a leash or a Terrier. The terrier will most likely be pre-occupied with his surroundings, not noticing the owner at all. And there is the Labrador who will check in with the handler the moment the handler makes a sound or moves. The *fight drive* is based on defense and will indicate if a dog is prone to defend himself when he feels threatened. You do not want a dog with a high fight drive who seeks conflict, but a dog which prefers to withdraw from the situation as to avoid conflict. A dog with high fight drive will have a greater tendency to guard his territory, toys or food and will be less likely to tolerate grooming and touch. Especially with children involved. The *flight drive* is also a defense drive but a great value to a family dog. A dog will be safer around children when they are more motivated to retreat in a kid-free zone, than engage the child in conflict. Some dogs with a high flight drive may submissively pee when they are a puppy but they will most likely grow out of this. The *play drive* is a great drive for family dogs to have. They love to play and engage in activities with the family. Though puppies love to play, this type of play is often based on looking for boundaries around them instead of having a truly high play drive when they grow up.

We covered the older dog in detail, so lets review how to choose a puppy or young dog. This can be a great idea for young families. A puppy can grow up with the children and have a higher "cuteness" value than older dogs. A few points to consider when adopting a puppy from a shelter:

> Some shelters spay their pups at a very early age which can increase a risk of incontinence. A study at Texas A&M University Surgical Sciences within the College of Veterinary Medicine included 1842 dogs in their study period. They followed these pups long-term and found that puppies who were spayed before the age of 3 months old had the

greatest risk for urinary incontinence. Medical treatment was required to assist in potty training. It does not happen often. It is something to be aware of if your puppy is not progressing at a normal pace in potty training. If you suspect a delay in potty skills or your pup has odd accidents contact your veterinarian for help.

➢ Puppies that were kenneled in shelters for some time could have a set back in potty training skills. Be extra consistent in working out a plan with potty training at home. Results will follow soon.

➢ Not knowing the background of the puppy you have to focus extra on socializing your puppy.

Socialization can make all the difference in raising a content family dog. Dogs raised in the same litter can end up on the opposite side of the behavior spectrum. It all depends how much they were socialized within the first year of life. If a puppy only sees the backyard when he grows up, compared to his sister who followed the family around with every outing, you will get two completely different puppies. The litter mates which were exposed to the big world learned how to problem solve, cope with stress, use communication signals to avoid conflict, bite inhibition skills and learned how to handle new situations when growing up. You have to prepare your young dog for life and that is a time commitment. You have to work with your puppy through different stages of development and preferably keep working with your puppy until he is at least a year old. While he grows up he will have to work through several fear periods in which he suddenly is more cautious about things. Be patient and continue to help him through these challenges. That first year of extra time investment in your dog will pay off in the long run. Socialization is not a well understood concept with first-time dog owners in the USA. The indisputable fact is that most dogs within the USA will never leave their property, fenced in backyards, invisible fencing or whatever acreage they live on. The abundance of land has made dog owners choose the easy route in exposing their dog only to the home property and never teach the dog to understand what is out there in the big world. I know the difference as I grew up in The Netherlands and can compare the American dog owners with the Dutch. The Netherlands is a tiny speck on the globe where citizens do not have the luxury of large property. Dogs are walked several times a day. Daily dogs will go shopping with the owners. Twice a day they will help pick up the kids from school. Or accompany the owner on a walk to mail a letter at the post office. Often you will see a dog waiting patiently outside the bakery tied on a leash in a down position, as mom or dad is buying some fresh baked bread for the family. Another challenge dog owners face in the USA is that everywhere you go, you have to include your car unless you really want to take a long stroll around the block. Stores, malls, post office or other destinations are never next door. You will seldom see dogs accompanying their owner. If they do, the dog stays in the car and never meets new people. It is not uncommon to see a dog in a restaurant in Europe. You may not even notice the dog. He is well socialized, behaved and curled up under the table while the waiter gently slides a bowl of water under the table. Different cultures, same canine species, though one society integrating their pet in every detail of their lives and in the other society they receive a completely different role. Guarder of property, companion at home and only in some cases a dog becomes a sports athlete with a devoted owner by his side. The fact is that people live further apart from each other in the USA. With this comes the extra challenge for your dog to meet new people each day and learn early on how to cope with challenges in life. So what does socialization include? Your dog has to learn to appropriately respond to all kinds of stimuli around them. A short checklist may give you an initial idea of what is involved;

   ✓ Exposure to adults
     (different ethnicities, different ages, gender,
     different clothing from bulky hunting gear to
     Halloween dress up, man with beards,
     sunglasses and more).

Halloween costumes

✓ Exposure to children.
(strollers, crawling babies, crying, group of children playing)

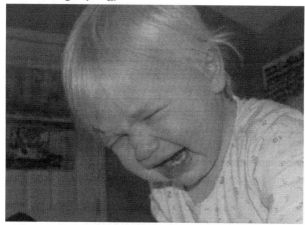

✓ Exposure to animals. (cats, dogs from big to small, fluffy covering eyes to wrinkly faces, life stock, wildlife, birds)

In memory of Koby; friend to the neighborhood and helper in socializing our dogs.

✓ Exposure to environment. (slippery floor, busy parking lots, school parking lots, pet store, bike trail, groomer, veterinarian, boarding kennels, traffic, noises)

Choosing the right dog for your family involves making many choices. But we live in a great country with professionals who can help you. Veterinarians, dog obedience trainers or behavior specialists can all give you additional help to make a choice based on facts. I have experienced the cutest dogs with horrific attitudes and ugly dogs with the sweetest predisposition you can imagine. Do not let your emotions take control. I know how tough that can be, let alone for a first time dog owner. Involve the whole family and make it a fun quest to find the right dog. But do not let your children make the final decision. I understand as a parent the power of seeing your child smile. But I would encourage you instead to create smiles based on spending quality time with your children. Of course your son or daughter will tell you that they are forever grateful if you would pick this or that puppy. Try walking through a pet store with your kids where they sell puppies. Yep, that is not a good idea. The smiles you receive from giving your child what they want are short term. The smiles you receive for playing games with your children, chasing a football in the yard, making wild flower bouquets together, reading stories or quiet cuddle time are smiles that change the heart of your child forever.

"To err is human, to forgive, canine."
Unknown

4   WHAT IS PROBLEM BEHAVIOR?

"What exactly is problem behavior?"; A great question to ask when a dog is around your child. Often dogs will do the cutest things while dog professionals would cringe at the thought of a dog behaving that specific way. If your dog displays any behaviors which are covered in this chapter, it would be wise to consult a professional trainer to help you modify the dogs' behavior. You do have to understand that a dog does not show wrong behavior. (unless the dog has a neurological disorder) But a dog *responds* to his surroundings. He communicates and responds to what happens near him. He may show unwanted behavior in our eyes which is a different issue and has to be addressed in training. But you have to keep in mind that a dog is an animal with a different thought process than we have. With that said I do agree that we have many things in common with a dog. We both function better in a community instead of being alone. But when it comes to hierarchy and body language we often fail compared to the dog. We have moved away from nature through time. I would recommend your reading the book *Last Child in the Woods* by Richard Louv. You will find the facts in how we increasingly deal with a

nature deficit disorder as a society. As we have become numb to nature it explains why as dog owners we are unable to pick up dog language very easily. The closer you are to nature, the easier it will become.

Chasing

Dogs often love to chase or to be chased, especially when they have a toy in their mouth. But chasing your children or being chased by children can lead to problems very quickly. Either side can get carried away in playing. When adrenaline sets in your child or dog no longer bases play on thoughtful actions. They are starting to react to each other which will make it even more risky. It starts with giggles from the kids and ends with a child on the ground in tears. The dog bumped into the child or used an ankle bite technique which some herding dogs use. Children love to chase a dog but it does not help you train your dog appropriate behavior. It will be a challenge to teach a dog to come if he learns that being chased is a lot more rewarding! Some children love to take a toy and have the dog run after them. Again, anything that involves chasing is asking for trouble. In this case you have to step up as a parent and either bring the dog in a kid-free zone to allow the children to play, or provide your children with a different activity. If you take a walk in the woods with the family it might be an idea to give the children something constructive to focus on to prevent them from running around and getting the dog all worked up. You can play different games that do not involve running around. You can play Sherlock Holmes and locate wildlife foot prints following them around. Or find bugs and identify them as to study their habitat. If your kids need some time to run then keep your dog on a leash. It prevents accidents if he is prone to chase the kids.

Resources

There are different resources in a dog's life. Some of which he puts a high value on or some of which he may not care about at all.

Resources include food, toys, chew bones and treats. To be absolutely safe, do not allow your child to approach a dog who has resources in his vicinity. You can notice if a dog has resource guarding tendencies by how he responds to you when you approach him. Does he try to block you by moving his shoulder or hind quarters into your path? Does he start eating or chewing faster and moves his mouth closer towards your hand as to warn you? Does he pick up his valued resource and walk away with it as you hear him say; "mine mine mine!"

Does his body freeze up? Does he growl or lift his lips? Or stare at you through the corner of his eye? There are many subtle ways through which he will warn someone not to come too close to him. Young children do not have the ability to discriminate these behaviors. We have to prevent these situations from happening as a child will be bitten when warning signals are ignored.

Guarding

Dogs can be very sensitive to the mood within the family. If there is tension they will pick up on it. Kids fighting, mom and dad arguing or parents arguing with the kids, it all comes down to tension. Some dogs may even feel the need to protect your child from threats. This could be a verbal reprimand when you tell your child to stop doing something naughty. A physical threat could elicit a defensive response in your dog. If you grab an arm or spank a child you might unknowingly provoke a reaction in your dog. Do you ever notice that your dog walks in between you and your son or daughter and stands still blocking your way? Some herding breeds may actually gently push a child away from danger with their body. When a dog starts to push your child with his body, blocking you from getting to your child or always mingle in when you reprimand your child, then it is time to evaluate his behavior.

I remember Abram. He was a huge German Shepherd who came to our home after no longer being able to stay with his family. He started off as a small sweet puppy and turned in a king who ruled his family. Abram demanded to be number one and due to his size it was not easy to gain his respect. I was able to turn him around and we became inseparable. He actually ended up becoming a police dog where he could use his skills. As his bloodline was focused on work skills one thing was ingrained in him. Herding my children was his specialty. I kept a close eye on his behavior. One summer day I was in the backyard watering the plants. My daughters were playing and chasing the stream of water in attempt to get their clothes wet. It is the small things in life that children enjoy; they remind us adults that we take life too seriously at times. Abram was hanging out in the yard. He made some poor attempts to catch a chipmunk. Suddenly he was distracted by the girls and I noticed him ever so subtly walk into the area where the girls were playing. With great poise he walked sideways and guided my girls away from the water by using his body to block them. A beautiful sight to see, but I did not allow it to continue too long.

Punching

To elicit a response, dogs sometimes punch each other with their muzzle. It is a quick punch aimed at your hand or body. The opposite of this behavior is when your dog gentle puts his muzzle under your hand and nudges it for attention. A muzzle punch is a more aggressive way of communication. It can happen in play or a warning when a dog feels threatened. Be aware of this behavior when your dog does this with your children. If it happens distract the dog with a jolly voice and remove him from the vicinity of the kids. It is a sign that the dog is no longer in thinking mode but in a reactive mode which can be risky. Often a dog who loves to play and gets carried away will display muzzle punching.

Stalking

Herding dogs may stalk due to their deep ingrained need to herd sheep. They may not mean anything harmful by stalking, but with some dogs it can be a severe warning signal for trouble. Stalking in combination with a high prey drive has to be evaluated by a professional. They can offer a training and/ or management plan for you and your dog.

Physical

Physical contact like petting or cuddling can be very soothing. But at times you have to be aware who initiated it. It may look sweet when a dog comes and cuddles with you on the ground. They love standing on top of you, or even laying on top of you. But it can get out of hand. If you do not control your dog through leadership and mutual respect your dog will turn the cuddles into pushing you around. These dogs may even clasp a child between their paws as if they are hugging the child. Be very careful not to put human emotions to dog behavior. It may look cute when a dog embraces you with his front paws on your shoulders. But it is very risky to allow this behavior around children. A dog will push a child to the ground and not respect personal boundaries to the point that they may receive the wrong signals when a child tries to move away.   Make sure whenever you cuddle with a dog you are the one who takes the initiative and are in full control of the situation. Rough housing is never appropriate.

Conflict

Behaviors which create conflict between your dog and your child is a cause for concern. It is up to the parent to resolve them and not the child. The following are examples of potential conflict:

1) Dog stealing food

2) Dog walks around with stuffed animal

3) Dog drags Barbie dolls by their hair

4) Dog stands in front of the door, blocking the way for everyone. With the kids putting shoes and coats on it can become very chaotic by the door.

5) Dog sleeps on couch during TV time.

Blocking

Dogs communicate with their body. Charles Darwin (1872) described in his book *The expression of the emotions in animals and human* that there are general messages we all send with our body. A stiff-legged movement and posture, upright and strong presence, is the language of dominance. If you notice your dog try to block your way or stands in front of your children with a dominant presence be aware of the situation. The dog that stands in front of a child with this posture and yet completely ignores the child is a safety risk. This will occur especially when a strange dog on a leash meets a child accompanied by a mom or dad. This dog signals that you have to respect his space and not invade it. The dog will not even glance at or acknowledge the child but acts as if he is alone on the planet. Keep your child away from this dog! Or if your own dog tends to do this and uses his body to push your child out of his path or blocks anyone from walking by, it is time consult a dog trainer. Dogs need to respect your space and not the other way around. If I am not alert to the situation, our dogs have the bad habit to forget about the kids when a toy is involved. When I get ready at the front door to get the dogs out I often witness a contest between the dogs and the kids. Who can come to the door the fastest! It is not a good thing. The kids end up being steamrolled by the dogs. My children are in no position to break up the dogs from running or pushing them out of the way. It is my responsibility to first put the dogs in a stationary position while I get the kids ready for a walk. When the kids are all dressed then the dogs are leashed by me to go out. It is my responsibility alone. As our dogs are retired service dogs I know the shortcomings of having high drive working dogs at home. They need extra exercise and mental stimulation. It is not a good fit with children around. But having leadership over your dog is the key to success.

"If you pick up a starving dog and make him prosperous,
he will not bite you; that is the principal difference
between a dog and a man."
Mark Twain

5   SAFETY SKILL STORIES FOR CHILDREN

The STORM project started in my own home many years ago after my first daughter was born. I learned how story telling is essential to teaching children instead of laying out the rules each day. If you want to help your child to understand dogs better then visualize a situation, and allow time for role playing which makes learning more interactive and effective. I gathered a few stories of our own dog Storm. These are stories based on truthful events and can provide some fun bedtime discussions. Each story ends with talking points to discuss safety issues with your child. After you have done this for a few days it would be a great idea to take your kids to a local library and find story books about dogs. Make up your own talking points after each story. Picture books help to visualize what you try to teach your children. You can even make up stories if you have a talent for this. Another idea is to ask your children to come up with stories together while you incorporate safety issues. It will bring tons of giggles and opportunities to teach about dog interaction and safety. Another idea is to allow your child to make a drawing of a story or a situation which is relevant to safety issues. The sky is the limit.

Stormy-puppy

It was a cold December day in Michigan. The snow was blowing so hard that you could not see the road in front of you. We drove on the dangerous roads to meet Storm for the first time. There he was sleeping in between his brothers and sisters. Storm was the smallest one of all. The moment we walked up to his bed he woke up. He sneaked away from his sisters and came to greet us. It was time to take him home. Tessa was so excited. She had cleaned her room and put down the special dog toys for Storm so he would not chew on her Barbie dolls. Dana her sister loved to play with Storm and lay on the ground like a doggy. But what do you think happened? Storm thought that she was a puppy and he pulled on her hair thinking it was a tail. And he would jump on her face to show her how big and strong he was. This hurt Dana so she decided to play different games with Storm. She always loved to run really fast and beat her sister. When Stormy saw Dana running he thought that that was a lot of fun and he chased her. He wanted to try to stop Dana and started jumping and grabbing her with his mouth. Dana fell and hurt her knee really bad. Her dad picked her up, gave her a big hug and told her that she has to play different games with Storm. Because dogs do not play the same way that we do. Her dad would teach her how

to play hide and seek with Storm. He did this so well that when Storm grew big he turned into a real super hero. Dana's dad and Storm helped police to find people who were lost in the woods. They had many adventures together. With Storm's first Christmas day the whole family sat around the tree excited to open their present. Tessa was so excited to get her first computer game. She did not want to share it with any one. She would get angry if her sister Dana would try to take it away. You know that Stormy did the same thing!? If he had a toy or a dog bone in his mouth or next to him, he did not want anyone to take it away either. He would get angry just like Tessa. Then Tessa and Dana learned not to ever take away food or toys from Storm because he loved them so much. When Tessa had a bad day at school she would always tell Storm about it and it would make her feel better. He was her best friend. Though Tessa and Dana had to learn what dogs like and do not like, it helped Stormy and them to become very special friends.

Talk about the story through the following talking points;

1) Do you like to share your toys?
2) Are you allowed to take a toy away from a dog?
3) Do you like to share your happy meal?
4) Do you think your dog will like to share his food and treats? Why not?
5) If your dog jumps on you do you push him away or do you tell mom and dad about it first?
6) Why can you not play with a dog when you are by yourself?
7) What happened with Dana in the story when she tried to run and go faster than her sister?

Bear

It was a warm summer day. The sun was shining and Tessa's dad was outside mowing the lawn. Suddenly he heard a noise. "What was that"? He thought. He looked around and there, right behind him, was a little black puppy. He was all alone and the puppy was scared. Each time Tessa's dad wanted to catch the puppy, the puppy walked away. Then he decided to stand very still and not look at the puppy. And something very special happened. The little black puppy carefully walked to him and started sniffing him. Tessa's dad slowly petted him and the puppy then knew that he no longer had to be afraid. Storm came outside to get to know his new friend. Dogs can talk better to each other because they know dog language better than we do. When Storm left the house to meet his friend both Tessa and her sister Dana came outside to see what was going on. They saw the puppy and got so excited that they screamed. Storm learned that when children make noise like that you do not have to be scared. But the puppy did not know this. You know how loud girls can be right? What do you think the puppy did? He was so scared he was hiding behind their dad. Their dad told them to do the same thing as he did so the puppy would not be so scared. It worked!

The puppy walked slowly to Tessa and Dana, and they became special friends. They named him Bear. Because he was so soft he felt like a little bear cub. Bear grew up to be a big dog, but he learned that people can be very nice. Storm taught Bear how to behave around other dogs and became his best friend.

Talking-points

1) *What made the puppy scared?*
2) *If you see a dog loose outside what do you do? Run after it to catch it or go tell your mom or dad that there is a loose dog?*
3) *Why is it better not to stare a dog in the eyes?*
4) *Do you like it if someone stares at you?*
5) *When a dog tries to hide from you, do you try to follow him or is it better to leave him alone?*
6) *Remember never to walk to a dog, but let the dog come to you. How can you see if a dog is scared?*

Bear in real life. He found a great home.

Storm the super dog. It was a cold winter day. Storm had to go with Tessa and Dana's dad on a very important mission. A hunter was missing in the woods, nobody knew where he was. Storm was trained to find people. He loved to do his job. Storm's dad and police officers went into the woods to find the missing hunter. Storm used his nose to smell. Dogs use their nose to find out where they are and to find things around them.

They can even smell the dirty socks that you hide under your bed. (Can you smell your dirty socks? ☺) Storm would run so fast in the woods he did not always look where he walked, he only used his nose. He was a real super dog. They worked all day long to find the hunter and then we heard the good news on the radio. Storm's team had found the hunter! He had hurt himself when he fell out of a tree! If it was not for Storm and his team no one would have found him. After a long day of work Storm went home with his owner and cuddled up in a warm blanket. He was really tired. At home he ate so much food his belly was as round as a balloon. While Storm fell asleep on his bed, Dana and Tessa came home from swimming lessons. They were so excited to see Storm they wanted to go to him and cuddle. But Storm did not like that at all! They woke him up while he was sleeping! So he walked away from the girls, he just wanted to be left alone to sleep. Tessa's dad told them to leave him alone and that tomorrow they could play with him again after school. So Tessa and Dana went to bed and could not wait for the next day to play with Storm again.

Talking-points

1) *Is it a good choice to touch a dog when he sleeps?*
2) *Do you like it if your mom or dad wakes you up at night?*
3) *Why did Storm walk away from the girls?*
4) *When a dog is tired or hurt they want to be left alone. How do you know if a dog likes to play again?*
5) *Can you play with a dog without asking mom or dad first?*

Storm is getting ready for his search mission.

The couch. Storm is old now. We found him a new friend whom he could teach to be a search dog just like him. That is how Jesse joined our family. Jesse the spotted dog loves to run. She is the fastest dog in the whole city. She loves to be outside and chase the squirrels. And after some fun play time the first thing she would do when she came home was jump on the couch. She would stretch out and her legs would be as long as the couch. When the kids came home from school, Jesse would still be sleeping on her favorite couch. One day Dana came home from school and wanted to watch TV. She loved to watch Nickelodeon but there was no place to sit. Jesse had taken the whole couch to herself! So Dana walked to Jesse and tried to push her off the couch. But you know what happened? Jesse became very angry! She growled and her eyes looked very mean. Dana walked away to find her mom. Jesse the dog knew she made a very bad choice and quickly walked away to hide. Dana learned that you can never tell a dog to get off the couch. Mom and dad are the only one who can tell a dog to do something. That is because they are bigger and dogs have learned to listen to them. So if your dog is on your bed or on the couch and you want him to move, find your parent to ask help.

Talking-points

1) *Is it a good choice to push a dog?*
2) *Do you like to be pushed?*
3) *If a dog is sleeping on the couch, or a bed, what do you do?*
4) *Did Dana run away to ask her mom for help or did she walk?*
5) *What would have happened if Dana was running?*
6) *Is it better to run or walk when a dog is nearby?*

THE TREE   What does a tree look like? It has branches, a trunk and roots. A tree is so strong and quiet that when a dog runs by he will not look at the tree. Have you ever seen a dog bark at a tree or try to push it over? No that is silly. But sometimes dogs are loose and run around in the woods or near your home. If you ever see a dog that is loose when you walk to school or play at a friends house you can play a fun game called "stand like a tree". This is what you have to do. You stand up straight with your feet on the ground and pretend you are growing really big roots into the ground. Your hands are like the branches, and to keep them safe you have to fold your branches together by clasping your hands together in front of your body. Can you do that? Then use your eyes to look at your toes and see if they are starting to grow a root into the ground like trees do. But you have to stand completely still, hands down, no talking and see who can last the longest. You can even count to the highest number that you know. And while you pretend you are like a tree, the dog that is walking loose around you will walk away and you are safe. You then slowly walk away to a safe adult. You can practice this game when you are taking a walk in the woods with your family and your dog is running around. You don't want him to bump you over right?

Talking-points

1) *You are playing football with a friend, or are doing hopscotch on the drive way. Suddenly a dog comes and joins in the game and is getting really excited. What do you do?*

2) *Do you start giggling and push him away or do you stand like a tree?*

3) *You are making a snowman outside and a dog grabs the hat of the snowman. What is safer to do?*

4) *Chase the dog, yell at him to get it back or tell an adult and just let the dog keep the hat?*

Activity idea; *Draw a large tree and find pictures in a magazine of dogs that are off the leash, playing or running around. Cut out the pictures and glue them around the tree.*

ROCK.

It is evening time and you want to watch TV. You are on the ground and your dog wants to play. There comes your dog and starts to step on you and pulling on your pants. He thinks you are his toy! To train your dog to stop that naughty behavior you have to pretend to be a rock. You curl up in a ball and cover your face with your hands and lay as still as a rock. Now your mom or dad can teach the dog to leave you alone and choose to play with real toys. You can help your mom and dad train your dog!

Talking-points

1) *You are at a friends house and are walking around with a plate of warm yummy pizza in your hands. The dog comes, pushes you over and the pizza falls around you on the ground. The dog starts eating it. What do you do? Push the dog away and grab your pizza, or do you let the dog eat the pizza and lay very still until an adult comes to take the dog away?*

2) *You have friends over to play. They want to play with your dog. What do you do? Ask a parent first or do you just start chasing the dog around?*

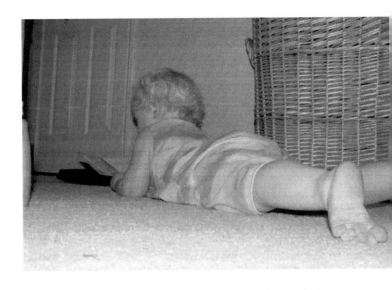

The dog has to stay away from these children
and respect their space.

"Scratch a dog and you'll find a permanent job."
Franklin P Jones

Training a dog to reach his fullest potential is very rewarding for both owner and dog.
In memory of my buddy; Brutus Augustus vd Vastenow

6   TRAINING PLAN FOR YOUR DOG

Dogs are not born with a built-in instinct on how to respond to children. They often perceive child play as a threat. But you can help your dog to cope with the communication gap. You can teach him to understand different kinds of physical contact like hugs or being grabbed by the neck. And help your dog understand to not interpret them as a threat. The importance of training can not be overemphasized. People come to me for help only after the problems have multiplied to the point that the dog has to be re-homed. This does not have to happen. Invest time in training. Learn to observe your dog. If at all possible become aware of your dog's breed background. Herding dogs are very alert to any movement. Some families have decided to get a small dog in the hope that small dogs can only bring small problems in the home. Often small dogs are not perceived by children as a dog, but more as a stuffed animal. This gives an extra challenge as children do not realize that these little furry friends are actual dogs. If you have a hunting breed in your home it may be an uphill battle to stop them from stealing the kids' toys. Then you have the Rottweilers and Pitbulls which have gotten a bad name in society for their aggression. Yet these breeds have very special character traits.

A training plan includes:

1) Socialization and basic commands
2) Building leadership over your dog based on respect and trust.
3) Teach handling and grooming skills.
4) Impulse control and bite inhibition training.
5) Exercise strategy
6) Focus training
7) Behavior evaluation
8) Baby boundaries
9) Games and constructive ways to play

Socialization is the most important part of your young dogs' life. Young dogs grow and will face critical periods during which they need to learn many skills. This process of socialization takes place mainly during the first year of a dog's life. Their whole life it will be important to bring your dog into the world and conquer challenges together. It builds a relationship with your dog. Exposing your dog to controlled situations in which he can grow mentally will develop his brain in such a way that he will learn to cope with stress more appropriately. Socialization will refine communication skills, help the dog relate and increase problem solving skills. Through reckless breeding we are faced with dogs who do not communicate well. They are not in-tuned with the people and dogs around them. Training will help them build these skills, though the ultimate way for a dog to learn is to interact with a mentor dog. Dogs have to be exposed to other dogs, they have to grow up in an environment in which they can learn and build self esteem. It is unfair from our stand point to push our dogs into situations which they can not handle. Not every dog can cope with pressures and may "suddenly" snap in the eyes of owners. But in reality the dog had already tried to cope with the situation for a long time. Well socialized dogs will be able to understand children better and grow into great family companions who can handle impulsive children. There are dogs which are specifically trained to help autistic children. These dogs will gently lie on top of a child to calm him or her. Being squeezed releases chemicals in the brain which help to calm down. They are trained to understand the need of a child. It has a calming effect on a child for example to hold the ear of a dog as to get an input from her surroundings while they walk together in a busy store. But these dogs often had to learn these behaviors and have an inherited balance within which allows them to be touched in ways other dogs would feel threatened.

A great way to help socialize your dog is to find a doggy daycare nearby. A dog daycare is a facility where you can drop off your dog during work hours. You pick up your dog the same day. While you go about your day, he/she will be in good hands. You can go to work, shop, visit your doctor or stay home without your dog. A good daycare is not just a social hang-out for your dog, their mission is to build awareness in dog socialization and the need for exercise. The role of group play at a dog daycare is;

- ✓ Refining communication skills.
- ✓ Since not all dogs have the exact same display and signals in play, your dog builds language skills and self esteem through communication.
- ✓ Your dog will learn not to overreact when exposed to a well balanced mentor dog. These dogs teach your dog calming signals. They will respect personal space and help your dog build trust.

- ✓ Your dog will learn appeasement signals. How to use them in real life as to reduce the chance of conflict with other dogs.
- ✓ Your dog will learn body awareness. Balance, muscle tone and agility. Experiencing positive touch will influence the brain chemistry and enhance problem solving skills. This reduces stress and helps your dog cope with the big world around him or her.
- ✓ They work with dogs one on one to help them with people skills. Teaching them not to panic when restraint or groomed, and rewarding good behavior.
- ✓ Dog daycare will encourage a dog to use his natural instincts. Teaching the brain to problem solve. Scent detection puzzles and following tracks can help your dog use natural instincts resulting in a content dog overall.
- ✓ Established dog daycare programs will have designated mentor dogs which they know very well. They will use alpha character dogs to help young dogs with bite inhibition problems. Or may use older and calm dogs to help build self esteem in timid dogs.
- ✓ The exercise that a dog gets through play will make the dog content at the end of the day.

Exercise releases chemicals in the brain which makes you feel good. When you pick up your dog from daycare he/she will be calmer the rest of the day. This is of great value when the kids come home from school and the busy time of day starts as you get dinner on the table. A content dog makes a great family member.

Leadership by the owner is a foundational component to having a dog at home. Dogs will test the boundaries. Visualize a fence at the edge of a cliff. The fence is the boundary which keeps you safe from danger. You will have to inspect the fence often to make sure it is still solid. The dog does the same with you. A dog needs to feel security from you. Every second of the day, your dog talks to you with his body and is looking for a response from you. We often fail to communicate back as we are not aware of the signals that we give to our dog. Dogs have a wide variety of signals and rituals to share information. They have an exceptional ability to pick up cues from us provided by a gaze or even pointing. (Miklosi 1998). Dogs can become very socially attuned to their family and will be able to determine if you are in control of the family pack or not. I am not talking about forcing your dog in an alpha roll flat on the ground to get your point across as a leader. What I mean is to use subtle language all day long communicating to your dog that you have full control over the situation. Yelling, frustration and anger in any situation are signs of weakness. The calmer we are within and portray that we are in charge, the more the dog will pick up on that. Some dogs are alpha dogs from the day they were born and will need additional training to learn to respect you or they will become unruly and start taking over control. They will ignore you and demand your compliance to their needs. If you do not comply they will step in. I know of a dog which would wake up his owner in the early morning hours. If she did not get out of bed in time he would stand on top of her growling with a leash in his mouth. In another case I worked with a family who had a dog which would get the best spot on the couch. Every evening the whole family was sitting on the ground watching TV. Needless to say, obedience classes are a great way to become a team and grow mutual respect with these born leaders. How often do you interact with your dog during the day? This is an important question to ask yourself. The more you work with your dog during the day, the easier the training will become. Basic obedience exercises should be a part of your daily schedule.

Finding new skills to teach your dog and challenge him is the basis of becoming a team. Just letting your dog out in your fenced backyard without your presence is not going to enhance the bond between you both.

These dogs are getting used to a boat. We had a great time shaping this skill and became a team when we reached the final goal.....body recovery missions on the water.

Most dogs have a "beta" character and need to feel the presence of a strong leader around them or they will start building anxiety, stress, fear and further problem behaviors accompanied with them. Some subtle ways to reflect leadership to dogs are;

- Be consistent in all you do. If you do not want your dog to pull on a leash than do not only step in when you are on a hiking trail, but also take control when your dog walks from your front door to your car.

- Calm body language. Dogs are very keen in figuring out how you feel inside. If you have a bad day or are upset for any reason than that is not the time to train your dog. Your voice, speed of breathing and movement all signal your mood and often we are not even aware of it. Become aware of your body! Everything is information to your dog. Teach yourself more subtle ways to move with small and calm gestures. Are you able to stand still for 10 seconds without any movement? The calmer you are within the clearer you will be able to communicate with your dog, based on compassion, trust and mutual respect.

- Do not talk to your dog all day long. Try to use your voice sporadically which will make praise or reprimand much more powerful.

- Teach your dog to earn attention. Nothing in life is for free. Teach him to sit-stay for everything. (food, cuddle, toy, going out the door, going into the car, putting leash on, guests coming over etc)

Train **your dog to be handled** in ways children would interact. Imitating your child with awkward hugs, kisses in the face, unbalanced toddler walking, bumping into the dog by accident or tripping over him are some things that you need to teach your dog to cope with. Often dogs are very patient which children just like their inherent patience with puppies. But the number one rule is to never leave your child alone with a dog. Even when you are not present for a second your child may give the dog a spontaneous hug. A well socialized and trained dog is able to handle touch and sudden approaches. He will be able to handle unexpected hugs or kisses from a family member.

We all perceive the world around us in a different way. Our senses are in tuned with sound, smell and touch. Touch is one component with dogs which needs our attention. There are two components you have to focus on in training. One is the pressure with which you touch a dog. All dogs are unique and have a different threshold when it comes to being able to receive touch. As Labrador Retrievers are bred to hunt in icy conditions their skin is very insensitive. They often use their body so roughly without even noticing, you have to teach them to become more aware of their body. Compare the Labrador with a Miniature Pinscher, who are very in-tuned to being touched. If your dog tends to retreat when you pet him firmly on his back, he needs some help in training. You can help him perceive your touch as a positive experience by combining your touch with a positive reward. You can use toys, or treats which help their brain associate firm touch with a positive feeling. Just in case your child hangs on your dog's back pretending he is a horse, your dog will learn to be less reactive if he has a sensitive skin. Keep in mind that if your dog has underlying skin problems like allergies be aware that touch may feel like needle pricks to him. Nerve endings under the skin can be painful. To go to the opposite side of the spectrum, how do you train a dog with no body awareness or sensitivity to be gentle with kids around him? A great exercise is the "playground of higher learning" taught by Linda Tellington. She uses Feldenkrais therapy for people and applies the same concepts to dogs. Feldenkrais therapy is very effective to learn to adjust senses and become aware of your body as to decrease sensitivity to surroundings and feel more calm within. The second component of touch is teaching your dog to trust you while you touch different parts of his body. The massage techniques of Linda Tellington are a great way to help your dog trust you and completely offer himself to you. As most children are bitten when they pull on a tail, grab a dog without warning or share a passionate hug around the neck, these are areas in which you can help your dog cope. It is still wrong for a child to interact with a dog that way, but you can help your dog to not react defensively in the unfortunate occasion that it does happen. By reducing the threat level of being touched in those ways you can increase the chances that the dog does not bite out of self defense.

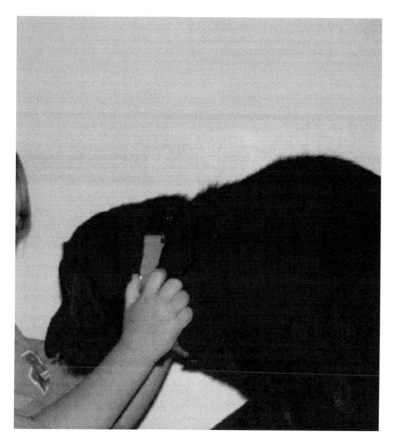

Not the right way for a child to hold a dog. The dog has nowhere to go and can't avoid eye contact to reduce conflict. This is Storm who is used to being handled and fully trusts the situation.

Socialization training includes teaching your dog soft **communication skills** instead of overreacting to situations. A young dog in our dog daycare program would be very rough with his mouth. He did not know how to use his mouth softly when he wanted to play or signal that he was frustrated by something. He would go straight into panic mode. So we helped him to use appeasement signals. These are signals which prevent a conflict from escalating. When I restrained him by holding his collar, he would overreact and mouth me very hard. But the moment he gave me an appeasement signal like a lick or looking away I immediately let him go. He learned that if he used gentle appeasement signals, the conflict would cease to exist. He was rewarded for using better communication skills instead of mouthing and being rude. *I do NOT recommend this training approach to the beginning dog owner.* But I described this training to give you an idea of what your dog is capable of learning. Not all dogs have the same start in life and have to learn new life skills. They may have been removed from their mom at a very young age and never experienced discipline for being too rough. They never learned bite inhibition or the feeling of being restrained in play with litter mates. Panic sets in before the dog has a chance to think through the situation. This behavior often happens with the first veterinarian visit. It is very important to find a good veterinarian with the patience to teach your young dog. You do not want to traumatize your dog with the first vet visit. Socialization comes into place to help our dogs to build social skills. Before you start training your dog to understand hugs, kisses, or touch, consult a behavior specialist to help you set up a training plan as each dog has different needs. *Do not start experimenting without professional help.* Not every dog has the ability to handle human contact at the same level. It will be wise to consult a trainer and evaluate what the dog's strengths are and also his limits. There are some basic training exercises which you can teach your dog to help him function within the family. Depending on your child's age they may be able to start training the dog too when they are in their pre-teens or older. But as a parent you have to do the foundational training first as to help your dog learn boundaries and prevent problem behaviors. With adolescent kids it is more a judgment call. Some teenagers are really good with dogs and have a talent to read the dog and train them. Though consistency is a pillar within dog training, which is not the strength of an adolescent as they can be very responsible one time and disengaged at a later time.

It all comes down to the adult who is the responsible party over the dog within the household.

EXERCISE

Problem behaviors often can be prevented if a dog has a daily outlet for his energy. Just taking a large dog for a leash walk around the block is not going to do it. Or even a half hour of

playing fetch is not going to help much. One component of exercise is that dogs need the ability to run full speed on a daily basis. The other component is to give them a job. Let their mind problem solve and work which will make them content. Think about it, when was your dog able to run full speed, stretching his legs for a full mile? When did your dog have something to do, hunt for a toy, carry something in a backpack or fulfill a task? Ideas like bike riding, pulling a sled, hiking, swimming, treadmill workout, doggy daycare, official training like schutzhund or competitive agility will make a difference in your dogs' life. A new dog sport is "Treibball". It is popular in Europe and a fun game for your dog and children. The dog learns to push large gym balls around, "herding" them into a goalie. The dog which pushes 8 large gym balls the fasted into a goalie wins. Children would love to help out with this exercise. Another great outlet for your dog's energy is tracking. Your child can hide and have your dog find him. This is actually a great game for the whole family.

FOCUS

Without a social connection with your dog you will not be able to keep your dogs' focus on you for a very long time. Especially when there are distractions around like playing children. Review your day and ask yourself how often did I interact with our dog? Dogs will be easily distracted with kids running around and you will loose control fast. A great way to teach your dog to focus on you is called the "watch me" command. Teach your dog that you are relevant. Each time your dog looks at you give him a simple command to follow up on, like "sit" and reward him. He will learn that nothing in life comes for free and that he will only get attention from you when it is through your initiative and not his. To teach him to look up at you, use a toy or a treat, or make silly sounds which pique his curiosity. The moment your dog looks up at you he receives his reward. When he is starting to understand what to do you can start increasing the duration before he receives his reward. When he learns to look at you for an increasingly longer time you can add distance between you and him. While you are standing in the kitchen teach him to respond to the command. This comes in handy when your children are playing or stumbling over the dog toys and you want to distract your dog to avoid any chances of conflict. When he learns to watch you under those conditions you can add distractions. Take it slow, step by step. Make sure to train each day for 10 minutes at a time morning, afternoon and evening. The more you repeat the exercise the faster he will understand what you ask of him. The more you have your dog focus on you during distractions, the better your control will be when he is off the leash around children. You need to become of value for your dog. The more time you spend with him the more reason he has to stay with you and not run away to do his own thing.

LEAVE-IT

A basic yet important command is "Leave it". I have encountered a few clients who had trained their dog to not pick up any food out of a hand. Only to pick it up off the ground. This can help your child to walk around safely with a cracker in the hand without being bothered by the dog. The disadvantage is that you can not reward by giving a treat from your hand. You will have to use different ways to reward in training. Clicker training is a great way to remove the treat from the training scenario.

HOLD-GIVE

Teach a dog the basic skill to give up a toy. It brings unwanted behavior, like stealing kids' toys, under a controlled command. Some dogs are so possessive over their toy or chew bone that it is wise to teach them to "give" but to also "hold". You put the behavior of holding something valuable under your full control and you teach the dog to become more dependent on your will as a leader. This can include food-bowl training. Contact a trainer if you suspect food-bowl aggression in your dog. A child may NEVER approach an eating, but you can include your child in the feeding routine. When a dog is solid in sit-stay, your child could put the bowl down and tell the dog to eat.

BEHAVIOR-EVALUATION

If you like to get to know your dog better and understand his strengths and weaknesses, it can be of great help to have a behavior specialist evaluate your dog. A social skills test can help you to get to know your dog better and determine how to become a team. A specialized training plan unique to you and your dog will help you connect with your dog. The more in tune you are with your dog, the safer it is for your children.

BABY-BOUNDARIES

You can use a doll, same size as a baby or toddler, to teach your dog to respect a child's space. In a positive way you work with the dog near the doll. Have the doll on your lap, simulate a diaper change on the floor or hold up your doll for "burp" time. These are great ways to help your dog learn that there are boundaries and he should not to step on the doll or lick it to death. It is not about correcting your dog, but to teach him to sit nearby and receive a fun toy or treat instead of being too close in the doll's face all the time. If you start correcting the dog all the time in the vicinity of the doll he is going to associate the doll with bad experiences. That is not what you want to have happen. testing of dogs in shelters or specialty clubs.

GAMES
Children can be a great help with games. Great dog games are tracking, hide and seek, scent training and teaching tricks like waving night night to the children when they go to bed at night. There are board games for the whole family where a dog is included too. Instead of encouraging your children to play tug of war or rough house, offer constructive play time.

HOW TO FIND A TRAINER or RESOURCES
Within the USA we have a couple of great organizations who have a network of dog trainers. You have to do your research through references to find an experienced professional but the following organization will help you start that process.

International Association for Canine Professionals
www.canineprofessionals.com

National Association of Dog Obedience Instructors
www.NADOI.org

Association of Pet Dog Trainers
www.APDT.com

Certification Council for Professional Dog Trainers
www.CCPDT.org

American Veterinary Medical Association
www.AVMA.org

Animal Behavior College
www.animalbehaviorcollege.com

Other great resources;

www.americanhumane.org
The KIDS project

www.avma.org/bluedog/default.asp
Blue Dog project

www.be-a-tree.com
A teacher's resource.

www.doggonecrazy.ca
A game for the whole family!

"The dog represents all that is best in man."
E. Charlet

7   OBSERVE YOUR DOG

So many warnings in this book, I know it can feel discouraging, but it is reality. We have to wake up as dog owners. Dogs are such special animals we still have to take on the responsibility to keep our children safe. It is often the child who makes the mistake of miscommunication. In this chapter I ask you to take time. Take a moment and stop what you do. Watch your child, her smile, or your sons' boyish naughty look before he climbs over the couch. Stand still and listen to your family around you. Observe your dog. It is an art which is forgotten in our society, to stop with our hectic lives and take a step back, quiet our mind and get in tune with our surrounding. Never will I forget my dog Guus, and how he taught me to step back a moment and observe. Guus is my retired service dog. He retired his duty as body recovery dog after my first two daughters were born. We accompanied our team on recovery missions with Law Enforcement throughout the country. Not an easy dog to have around my children. He was bred to work with a high drive to complete his task in life. His obsessions about resources like toys and his hunting skills were such that he was talented for his work but lousy at being around our daughters. He needed frequent breaks to retreat from the girls. Guus and I spent many hours a day together training and perfecting his search skills and my handling skills. (which needed more help then his search skills ☺) He excelled in his recovery work but he did not like to sit still and receiving cuddles. That was beneath him, so I never asked that of him. He preferred to chase a tennis ball for the girls, he could do that all day long. Never did I ever think what he would mean to my daughter Dana. One fall vacation my husband and I had a bright idea to go on a hike in the Porcupine mountains in the Upper Peninsula of Michigan.

We took Guus, our daughter Tessa who was 3 years old and our daughter Dana who was 2 at that time. Still in diapers but loved any adventure that we took her on. It was a beautiful fall day. The fall tree colors were at its peek. After an hour of hiking carrying out girls with a backpack we had to climb down an embankment. It was pretty steep but we thought we could handle it. I took Tessa down first and my husband had Dana in his arms. Guus was off the leash walking around us. Suddenly I noticed that he started pacing back and forth. He was so focused on Dana. A minute later while Dana was climbing down with her dad's guidance, Guus started circling Dana and nipped at her diaper. He kept repeating it. I did not instantly reprimand him because I knew him very well, something was wrong. Then I realized that he was concerned about Dana and wanted to herd her back up the embankment. It was a very special moment to see him so concerned about Dana. He did not want to hurt her so he used his front teeth only on her diaper to try to get her to safety. My husband and I listened to Guus' guidance and agreed that our hiking ambitions were a bit too much for our small children. So we headed back with a memory of how a dog can be an essential part of a family.

Take the time to get to know your dog. A great book to read about detailed human-dog communication is *How to speak dog* by Stanley Coren. This book will dissect each part of the dog and explain how he/she talks to you. The ears, eyes, body, hair, tail, face and vocalizations all speak to you. A great way to learn something is to teach. So why not incorporate your child in listening and observing what a dog is "saying"? A dog does not speak with only his eyes or mouth. He uses his whole body. His tail will let you know if the wagging is based on stress or excitement. If only the tip of the tail wags there is more stress or anxiety in your dog. If the entire tail wags, including his hindquarters, the friendlier your dog is in greeting and playing.

Cesar Millan, a best selling author and the Dog Whisperer on the National Geographic Channel, mentions "energy". There may be controversy around his approach to behavior modification, but I know he is right on the mark when it comes to describing the energy we all have around us. Leaders project a presence which comes from within. And you will be able to pick up on this energy when you learn to take time in your day and quiet your mind. Soak in what is happening around you. Our minds go from one topic to the other and we never stand still in the moment. A man whom I deeply admire is Brother Lawrence. A compilation of his writings is called *The Practice of the Presence of God*. He points out a great truth which I strongly believe is also a reason why we are unable to connect with our dogs. The problem is that our mind is always thinking about *what's next* or *ponders on the past.* He comes with a simple yet profound example in life. When you do the dishes at night after dinner, do you clean the dishes in order to get the kitchen ready for desert? Or as Brother Lawrence has taught me, are you able to do the dishes for the sake of doing the dishes?

What does this have to do with dog training? Everything! Our society is teaching us to complete one task after another. We never stop accomplishing and think about what's next. When we drive to pick up the kids from school our thoughts are with projects, to-do lists and dinner time in the evening. Do you ever allow yourself while you drive your car to just focus on driving and allowing your mind to marvel at nature that bypasses you at 60 mph? Or feeling your car touching the blacktop and not allowing your mind to focus on the shopping list for later that day? Have you ever just sat down and let your children play around you. You just let their sounds and movement go about around you. And in the same way observe your dog while the children play games in the living room. If you practice to live in the moment, you will start picking up this energy and will learn to grow the ability to listen to your dog and observe what he is telling you. Is your dog calm within while the children play hide and seek?

Even when the kids crawl near his dog bed? Or do you notice his eyes changing into a worried look as your son or daughter tries to hide underneath his bed? You will never notice these subtle changes in your dog if your mind is absorbed by future tasks and thoughts that have nothing to do with living in the moment. A dog talks to you all day long. But we have become increasingly numb to those signals as our world surrounds us with noise. Pagers, blackberry's, computers, tv's, radio's and to-do lists. We loose the ability to sit down and quiet ourselves within. Have you ever observed your dog during the day? The movement of his eyes, his tail, his muscle tone, the corner of his lips, tongue movement, ear movement, body postures, a dog uses all of these to communicate. Our society has pulled us away from nature and feeling comfortable with stillness. Start with one minute in a day to stop what you are doing and still your mind. Connect with your dog. Slowly build up this time.

As you may already know, a dog is a group animal. That is why they fit so well in our families. But dogs need a clear hierarchy in which to function. That will help them feel safe and content at home. Within this hierarchy at home, children have a higher social status than the dog. This is a tricky situation as children under the age of 10 do not have the ability to communicate their higher social status. That is why we as parents, teachers, dog owners have to step in.

As you learn to observe your dog and get to know him on a deeper level, you will also notice stress signals. These are crucial to understand. Before your dog has reached his limit he needs a break from the situation he is in. Stress signals are easy to pick up. Most dogs will walk away when they reached their limit. That is why it is so important to give your dog the room to retreat. When you are well in-tuned with your dog you will be able to remove him from the situation before he reaches his limit. This helps your dog gain trust in your leader skills. You may notice when a dog walks away from a stressful scenario that he shakes of his body. The dog shakes off stress as if he is drying his fur after a bath. This is a great signal that your dog went from emotional thinking and stress back into his calm self and ability to think clear again. You will see this happen in training too. A respected trainer Brenda Aloff does an excellent job in explaining when a dog is in thinking mode versus reactive mode. It all depends which part of the brain is engaged.

Signals of stress in the dog and levels of severity;
1. Dog yawns, licks his nose, blinks his eyes
2. Dog turns his head away to avoid eye contact. He may turn his head away moving his toy away from your child. Putting his paw on the toy as a way to guard it.
3. Dog turns his body away from your child to avoid conflict
4. Dog walks away and may even hide
5. Dog will become stiff, his muscles cramp up
6. Dog's front leg lifts up while he stands very still
7. Dog starts to stare, you can also often see the white of his eye
8. Growling starts
9. Snap or muzzle punch as a warning
10. Dog bites

When you notice any of the above behaviors you have to take steps to respect the dog's space and keep your child safe. There are different ways you can alleviate stress in your dog. With a foundation of a well socialized dog and daily exercise there are different things you can do. Your dog needs room to retreat in, in order to be able to remove itself from a tense situation. It may not always be possible to let your dog walk away to a kid-free zone. You can use a jolly voice to help your dog understand that the circumstances he finds himself in are not threatening and distract him while you coax your child away from the dog. The "Jolly Routine" is a term used by the renowned canine behaviorist William Campbell. It means the pet parent should "act" relaxed and happy or "jolly."

Jolly Routine directions

1) As your dog notices your body language and perceives a frozen body posture as tension or threat, relax your body posture and muscle tone. Be loose and wiggly. Talk in silly in high pitch tone. Your tone, not what you say, is important.

2) Dogs will mimic their leader. If your dog is responding fearfully to a person, animal, or object, then focus your attention and friendly body postures at whatever scares him to show you are not afraid or threatened by it.

3) Request a SIT, and if the dog can do it praise big, and if not, move the dog away from the situation, and find a way to get a SIT, so you can praise that instead of the tense postures.

DO NOT:

1) Yell, scold or punish the dog. To punish a dog adds tension and shows the dog that indeed the situation is bad.

2) Don't soothe the dog. It rewards the anxiety within him and has a counter effect.

A third way of alleviating stress in a dog is to take control of the situation and reflect your leadership. Either use the jolly routine or give your dog a simple command to follow up on. For example tell your dog to sit and praise him for complying. It helps his brain to re-focus on you and feel positive about the situation. Well socialized dogs will give clear warning signs before they would consider biting. In order for a pack of dogs to co-exist they want to avoid conflict. That is why dogs have such a great ability to tell us how they feel. But we need to learn to understand their language. Dogs will only bite if they feel threatened physically, or feel their social status is being compromised. Dogs do not display wrong behavior.

Observe situations in which a dog may become frustrated. A helpful command to teach your dog is "back away". When guests arrive at the front door, most often the family pet wants to be right in the middle of the excitement not leaving any room for the guests to come in your home. Another situation is where there is a boundary involved which is frustrating your dog. Boundaries can be a leash, fence, a car with an opened window or a window in your home through which your dog sees "intruders" on "his" property. The dog builds up frustration and will increasingly be motivated to take it out on anything that he perceives lower in status whenever the final drop hits him. Keep your children away from these scenarios. Give your dog room and keep your child away.

ACTIVITY for the whole family
Draw a funny dog on a piece of paper. Together with your kids find pictures in a magazine of happy, angry or fearful dogs. Glue them around the dog below. While you do this, talk with your children about how to recognize an angry dog versus a friendly dog.

"No one appreciates the very special genius of your conversation as the dog does."
C. Morley

8   RESPONSIBILITY

There are programs developed by different organizations to help children understand how dogs think. But as a parent and/or dog owner we have to understand that it is our responsibility ultimately to keep our children safe. You may not have a dog at home and do not feel comfortable with dogs, so how then do you teach your child the proper skills? Dogs are everywhere in society. As children explore boundaries at home the most likely child behaviors that result in biting are pulling a dog's tail, fur or paws according to research by Millot in 1988.

Our responsibilities involve awareness with;
  ✓ Story telling versus rules
  ✓ Need for involvement
  ✓ Health care and veterinarian visits.
  ✓ Sibling rivalry, tension between dog and child.
  ✓ Dog proofing the house and outdoors.
  ✓ Mood transference within family and dog.
  ✓ Role model as parent.

To just hold a set of rules in front of your child will not amount to anything. Children learn best through **story-telling** and visualization which brings the issue at hand to their thinking level. For example the concept of "sharing" is a daily concept that each child struggles with. You can use the following example to explain the problem that dogs have with sharing.

A conversation you could have about the concept of sharing; " Do you like sharing your Happy Meal? Why not? What do you do when someone sneaks up on you and grabs your Happy Meal? "

Use open ended questions as to encourage your child to think through how to answer. This can prevent a simple yes or no answer. After your child explains the situation and feelings, you then can explain that the dog feels the same way when you grab a toy or treat away from him. But a dog can not talk like a person can, so he may growl and even bite.

Another concept is "strangers". Most dogs will be confused and may even perceive it as a threat when a strange person walks straight at them. Children are not comfortable either with strange people who do not respect their personal space and get too close or follow them. Dogs perceive it the same way. That is why is it important to understand that it is safer to have a dog greet a child on the dog's terms.

If a child wants to pet a dog have the dog approach the child to sniff his or her hand after which the dog will decide if he is comfortable with the situation or not. If not, he will simply walk away. Some dogs will be disinterested in the child and will not even approach the child. Respect this decision and do not allow your child to approach the dog or force the dog into a greeting. It all comes down to being involved as a parent when your child and dog interact. To be more precise, you have to be actively involved. For example, reading a book while your dog and son or daughter play on the floor is not being actively involved. If your child wants to interact with the dog, you first take steps to have full control over the dogs' actions, after which you invite your daughter or son to join you in a game of fetch, hide-and-seek, trick training or other activities.

If you are afraid of dogs, then contact a dog trainer in the area to help you and your child hands-on to build self confidence in meeting dogs on the street. You do not have to love dogs, but it will help your children to be safer if they know how to respond when a strange dog walks up to them or when they play at a friends' house. Being involved as a parent means to be actively engaged when your child interacts with the family dog. Be alert to the body language of your dog and his whole demeanor. When you notice stress be vigilant. Yawning or avoiding eye contact tells you that the dog is not comfortable with the situation. It is a possible start of problems which can escalate. A well socialized dog will give you very clear warning signals and will be an open book to you on how he feels. The dog will learn that you have control over the children and can trust you in situations which are not ideal for him. Through observing your dog when you train him and interact with him through the day you will get to know what level of stress your dog is able to handle. If a dog sleeps on the couch all day in a quiet home, his brain will not learn how deal with chaos around him. You have to work with your dog. Doing obedience exercises, focus training (watch me command), and impulse training (teaching to be patient), teaches what stress feels like and how to turn off the adrenaline within. NEVER leave your child alone with a dog. Involvement is the key to bite prevention.

As a parent we have the responsibility to get to know the family dog well enough to become very keen to his or her needs. You will pick up any signals in case there is something medically wrong. Regular check ups with the **veterinarian** will ensure your dog is in good health and in a good state of mind. Pain, discomfort, vision loss can all play a role in the stress level of your dog. Some medical issues can be so subtle that you do not pick up on them fast enough. Consult your veterinarian about regular exams and what to look for in your dog. Ear infections can cause a dog to become irritable to the environment and touch. You will notice that your dog starts shaking his head as his ears may be painful or itchy. Some dogs may have impaired vision and could get spooked if they did not see something coming at them. Any type of infection can cause irritability, so there are many reasons to keep your dog in good health and include your veterinarian in keeping your dog healthy. If your dog receives medical treatment, consult your veterinarian for any possible side effects of medicine. There have been reports of behavioral changes in dogs due to medicine intake. Though the chances are very remote that your dog may respond negatively to a medical treatment, it is wise to educate yourself and ask for information from your veterinarian.

Sibling rivalry can happen within any family. Children already tend to compete for attention from mom and dad let alone if they have to compete for attention with the family dog. If a dog joins in, this rivalry may grow into a real problem. Kids can start acting out towards the dog or the dog may even respond to the tension between children. If your son or daughter acts up when the dog is around you, it would be wise to separate them and give the dog some time by himself while you have quality time with your child. When the kids are in bed may be the best part of the day to give the dog more attention and focus on training issues. If you want to train a dog you have to be mentally present. It does not help if you have to watch your child while you train your dog. Besides being distracted it will also create frustration and may you end up misdirecting your dog in training through incorrect timing of rewards or taking out your tension on the dog if he does not comply.

As days can become very busy it is not easy to also keep an eye on your child while your dog walks around the house. One of the things we as parent tend to do is to leave the child to make decisions which they are not old enough to take. We let our child solve a problem which involves the dog. This can cause very risky situations. Most dog bites are the result of conflict between the dog and the child If a dog is sleeping on the couch and your child wants to get a spot on the couch they will grab the dog to pull him off. Or your child walking around with a cracker and the dog is trying to snatch the treat. A child most likely will push the dog away or yell at him. Sibling rivalry is another problem where children tend to take matter into their own hands to resolve the conflict that they have with the dog. To avoid a situation in where you child has to problem solve teach your child to call you for help. Or if it involves food and you are not close, have your child simply drop the food and walk away to report the incident to you. If it involves sibling rivalry, you will have to step in before the rivalry even takes place and give the dog a break from the family.

Dog proofing your home can be a family project. Keep the toys in designated areas, no eating around the dog, and when the Thanksgiving Turkey is cooling off on the counter keep your dog away in a safe place. If your dog has a happy tail than keep him away from the coffee table when you have your coffee steaming hot ready to drink. Do not allow your dog to retreat in a corner of the living room while your child wants to play. Cornering a dog is not a good idea. If their stress level reaches a crucial point and the dog is cornered, he will revert to defending himself as there is no way out.

No dogs allowed by the table during dinner time. It avoids conflicts like stealing of food and nuisance begging.

A different part of dog proofing the home is to avoid any loose toys in the house. Designate an area at home where the kids play to keep the kids' toys away from the dog. This is a tough one I know. I have lost count how often I have been chasing a beheaded Barbie around stuck in between canine teeth. In the background my child is crying crocodile tears and my dog thinks it is all really funny since he is getting all the attention! Also consider dog proofing the outdoors. In light of child safety I would not recommend having your dog outside on a cable. If the dog sees a squirrel he will take off including cable and could hurt kids who are in proximity. If you have an outdoor kennel in which your dog resides often, it is in the best interest of the dog to not have him kenneled outside when the kids play in the yard near him. Especially breeds which belong to the American Kennel Club Working group, Terrier group or Herding group have a tendency to become very agitated when kids play and run while the dog is restrained. To avoid this happening keep your dog out of sight by building the kennel in a more appropriate area. Or keep the dog inside when the kids have friends over and play in the yard.

If you are using invisible fencing to enforce a boundary around your home be aware of some shortcomings to this system. As children are able to walk in and out without being aware of the boundary you have to educate your neighbors and your own kids where the boundary is. Teach them to respect this zone around the property as to not run back and forth thru it. Kids may not even do it on purpose as they play their games outside, but for the dog it is highly confusing and at times frustrating to see children run through the zone which for the dog is an area associated with punishment. Not all dogs will be as sensitive to this, but the breeds that I mentioned before within three different working groups have a higher susceptibility to becoming agitated under those conditions.

Mood transference is a common concept in the dog training world. Dogs can be very sensitive to how you feel or to any type of tension within the family. A dog is also a master of picking up any negative vibes from people who have the wrong intensions in mind or are simply scared. Any type of tension will influence your dog. Some more than others of course, but you have to be aware that when your dog is with you he or she will know what is going on sometimes even before you do. One of my dogs has the ability to sense things that I can not. He is so in tune with people that he can surprise me at times. He had a social youth and is fine with people of all ages, gender or background. Yet 1% of the time when there is someone near my children, not a direct family member, he starts to guard my children while being near this person. He will allow everyone near 99 times out of a 100 and suddenly he picks out one person whom he does not trust. Dogs have such an incredible ability to sense there is something wrong that this same behavior may occur within the home. Kids can quarrel, you may have an argument with your husband, or you are reprimanding your son or daughter for not doing their homework. Situations in which tension arises allow for stress to build up in a dog. Not each dog is as sensitive to its surroundings but it is possible for a dog to react to negative vibes in the home. They become unruly, loud, and naughty or sometimes start to bark at the person who has the loudest voice. Do not unload on your dog in these circumstances, nor let your son or daughter step in. But take a deep breath, calm your senses and distract the dog with a jolly voice towards his kid-free zone to give him a break and allow yourself to finish the discussion you had with a family member. Through time dogs truly become part of the family in every sense.

Some family dogs may even become protective over the children towards the parent. It has happened in class situations where I would work with a family and their dog became protective over their son without the parent noticing it. The mom asked her son to sit and settle down, while her dog subtly yet determinedly wedged himself between the mom and her son. The more serious she became towards her son, the more anxious the dog became. He started panting and licking the little boy, trying to interfere with the conversation that mom had with her little boy. Dogs can get worried when something is off within the family. Most dogs can cope with the change in atmosphere but some need a break from it. Dogs that can not cope with chaos within the family will show a *ganging up* effect. The dog will start to act out at the weakest link within the family. If you are not sure if your dog is displaying this behavior contact a behavior specialist.

Another responsibility we have as parent is to be a **role model** towards our children. We often do not realize how our dog watches us each second of the day. Just like what our children do right? But keep in mind when you reprimand a dog or do an exercise to teach your dog new skills, your child may want to do the same thing. If you use compassion and respect, your child will mimic these same skills and also treat a dog with respect. But when you as parent cross a boundary, you can expect your child to do so too. Through being a role model you are teaching your kids in a subtle way how to interact with dogs. I have learned this the hard way myself. After my dogs retired from their service work, it became increasingly difficult as a mom of 4 girls to spend quality time with my dogs. Through the years when a visitor drives up our driveway my dogs have become increasingly noisy to alert our family of the intruders in our territory. It must have slipped my mind those times to stay in charge of the situation and I yelled out the Dutch words *hou op* to my dogs. I now have my daughters use the same words when the dogs start to bark. Yes it is adorable when a 3 year old girl attempts to use a low voice and yell *hou op* but I know I failed as a role model in this case. It is funny how our own children teach us life skills, isn't it?! They are true gifts from God! As life has its seasons there will come a time where you have to step up as role model and teach your child about grief and loss. Puppies bring their unique challenges. But what do you do when your dog has reached the age to say goodbye? How do we prepare our children for loss? The aging process and the different stages of life of animal will help your child understand what real life is about. We can not protect our children from everything. If your dog is no longer able to live a quality life due to medical problems, the big step is to make the decision of euthanasia. I have been there. And as a parent we have to think about our children and help them understand what is happening. Never tell your child that they are putting the dog to sleep. This may result in nightmares as youngsters take everything so literally that they become afraid to fall asleep at night only never to wake up again. When it is time involve your child teach them grief is not easy to deal with but very real in life.

Do not take away the ability of your children to grieve, process what is happening and grow. Doggy heaven is very real! It is comforting to know.

Summary of safety skills to teach your child.

- Do not walk to a strange dog. Tell your parent or safe adult if you see a stray dog.
- Don't stare at a dog, look away. Even if your dog wants your cookie, just drop it on the floor. Dogs do not share.
- If a dog is on a chain, behind a fence or in a car, keep walking and do not talk to the dog. If your football ends up in the neighbor's yard, do not climb the fence to get it back. But ask a parent for help.
- Do not tease a dog. They do remember!
- If a dog knocks you over, you roll up and cover your face, pretend to be a rock.
- If a dog is loose around you and starts chasing you, freeze like a tree.

- Leave a dog alone when he sleeps, eats or chews on a toy. Never wake up a sleeping dog
- Always ask permission from your parent to play or pet a dog.
- Dogs don't like you on their back, if you like to climb on something go to a playground.
- Dogs do not like hugs or kisses in their face. Ask mom or dad first if your dog is trained to know what a hug or kiss means.
- If you have permission to pet a dog, let the dog come to you to sniff your hand. If the dog likes you and is friendly, tickle him under his chin. Do not try to pet him on his head.

"I'd rather have an inch of a dog than miles of pedigree."
Burnet

9   MEET & GREET A DOG

When you watch the television ads, often you will see a commercial with a family and a golden retriever as family member. Dogs have a significant role in society. Not only as companion but as sports athlete, service worker, protector, movie star, shepherd or therapy assistant. They are magnificent animals though not always fully understood. As dog owners we have to take responsibility to help children understand how to behave around our dog. When you take your dog for a walk around the block you will be confronted with either children who would either love to hug your dog, or some who may run away in panic. When there are no parents nearby I would not recommend having your dog greet a child while he is on the leash. Children are unpredictable. To keep children safe we have to look at both sides of the equation. You have the dog owner who is responsible and the child who has to learn how to respond to dogs in the neighborhood. Then there are the parents with their own unique role in the whole equation. They are the only ones who can prepare their child what to do when they meet a dog on the way home from school, or while playing at a friends house.

Dog-owner

Your dog may or may not like children. You may not even know how your dog responds to children if you do not have children at home. So what is the safest approach to encountering children on your daily walks? If you live in a sub division with lots of kids around, you have to determine if your dog is safe for the neighborhood. I do not take this lightly both as a mom and dog professional. I have experienced the difficult decision to euthanize a dog as he was a danger to the community. You may find yourself on a sidewalk with a group of kids begging to pet your dog. Honestly, lets evaluate this situation. Does your dog benefit from being petted by a group of strange kids, leaning over him, staring at him, invading his space? You may answer this with yes, if you consider the importance of socialization. But there is a difference in forcing your dog into an uneasy situation which he is not ready for. Instead set up a controlled situation with kids you know and include parents. If you want to socialize your dog the goal is to make it a positive learning experience, and not a survival exercise. The answer on what to do when you are approached by children you do not know to pet your dog? Keep walking and tell them maybe another time under different conditions. As a dog owner understand your dog, and the need for personal space. Your dog may be mildly nervous about children, but when a dog has restricted movement on a leash he will respond differently as there is no way to retreat from a threatening situation. Personally I never allow my children to approach a strange dog which is on the leash. I know it is an extreme point of view, but I want to be on the safe side. I mostly am more concerned about the owner who is unable to observe their dog and control it than my concern for the dog.

Parent

I could have kept this chapter really short as I do not allow my children to ever approach a dog even though the dog is on the leash. Having a dog on a leash is not an ideal situation for a dog to greet a child. I try to desensitize my children to the cute faces of puppies or older dogs. If they really want to greet a dog I take full control of the situation. I approach the owner, and observe the dog closely before I even allow the dog to approach one of my daughters. If the dog is calm and has a friendly disposition I will still stay right next to the dog while the dog greets my daughter.

The following is the most appropriate way for a meet and greet time;

1. Child asks parent if they could pet the dog, while keeping a safe distance.
2. Parent asks dog owner for permission to greet the dog.
3. If owner feels the dog will be ok with it, let the dog approach the child while the child holds her hand out for the dog to sniff. Have your child stand sideways to prevent a staring contest with the dog. I prefer this method as you give the dog a chance to make a choice and retreat from the situation. This is a safer approach than having a child approach the dog and cornering the dog between leash and owner. Worse yet is owners who hold the dog by the collar so the child can approach the dog to pet.
4. If the dog is interested to meet the child he will approach him or her on his own terms. As to not give any threatening signals to the dog, the best way to pet a dog is under the chin or on his cheek under his ear.

WORKSHOPS

If you are interested in a child safety workshop with your family, would like more information or set up a speaking arrangement about STORM™, *you can connect with me through my website.*

Jeanette Groner

www.nodog-leftbehind.com